"Forever Family Book 4"

By

ALL OF Us

Dear Family,

Well this is the last of the books, I just wanted to take a moment to remember how lucky and blessed we are to have one another. I Think this book is special because we all made this book possible by the loving memories we have shared. Let's work on making some new ones so we can make a book 5 ok? I have had a blast working on this gift for all of you. Looking at these pictures, made me feel as through Grandma, Grandpa and Dad, Uncle William, Aunt Viola, Uncle Walter are still alive, and they are! They live in our hearts. They are always here with us as we make new and wonderful memories. As I have said in the last three books, if we have any differences or grudges against one another, let's let them go. Life is to short. We are here to love one another, for whenever we love another person we touch the face of God. God has graced us with the love of family. We should always thank him for that. One day when God felt generous,

He looked down at me and smiled,

"Since I feel so magnanimous,

I'd like to give you something, child."

He asked me what I wanted,

I said, "Oh, really nothing more,

You've done so much already."

He said, "That's what God is for."

"You have been pretty good," He said,

I know there's not much that you seek,

I will pick a little something,

Just to make your life complete."

With great anticipation,

I looked forward to my gift,

I wondered what God had in mind,
That would give me such a lift.

"This gift," God said, "You realize,
Bears some responsibility,
So, if you accept my present,
You must be willing to agree...

"To offer unconditionally,
A section or a part,
Of more than half of you,
The larger portion of your heart."

"Okay, God," I answered,
"Since in You, I always trust,
I'll meet your obligation,
In the manner that I must."

To myself, I thought, wow, what a gift,

For so much of me, God's asked,

Now what could be so valuable?

That my share was more than half?

With both hands I sought my gift,

I still did not have a clue,

Then God put your hand in mine,

And said His gift to me was

YOU!

I Love you all. Please always know that...Please let us cherish the time God has granted us to be together. Oh and before I forget, No one out side the family have access to these pictures and books, they have not been created by the usual way I create my books to sell. I paid my publisher to allow me to only create 10 copies of these books for the family. I have all the pictures and no one else, so they are not being sold to the public and I am the only one that had access to create these books.

Love Patti

Dad

My girls and I....

Brian and Holly in Upstate N.Y.

My best friend and I in New Orleans

Brian Mom and I in 2007 I was sad cause that was first trip to N.Y. AFTER DAD PASSED...

19/12/2009

Me in 2009

New Years Eve 2009

New Years Eve 2009

Mom cooking ham.. New Years day 2010

Anthony having fun in fla

On our way to N.Y. in 2009

Great Grandma and Dad in F.l. wow this is an amazing picture!!!!!!!!!!

Anthony and the Easter Bunny

Anthony and Baby Jocelyn

Dad and Grandpa......

Grandma

Anthony and I waiting for a concert to start....

I think this is Grandpa's family but not
sure....

Cute one of dad and Uncle Joe....

Holly and I in 1990

Family Love.....

Grandpa and Grandma in Central Park 1952

Aunt Viola Helen and ?????

Grandpa....

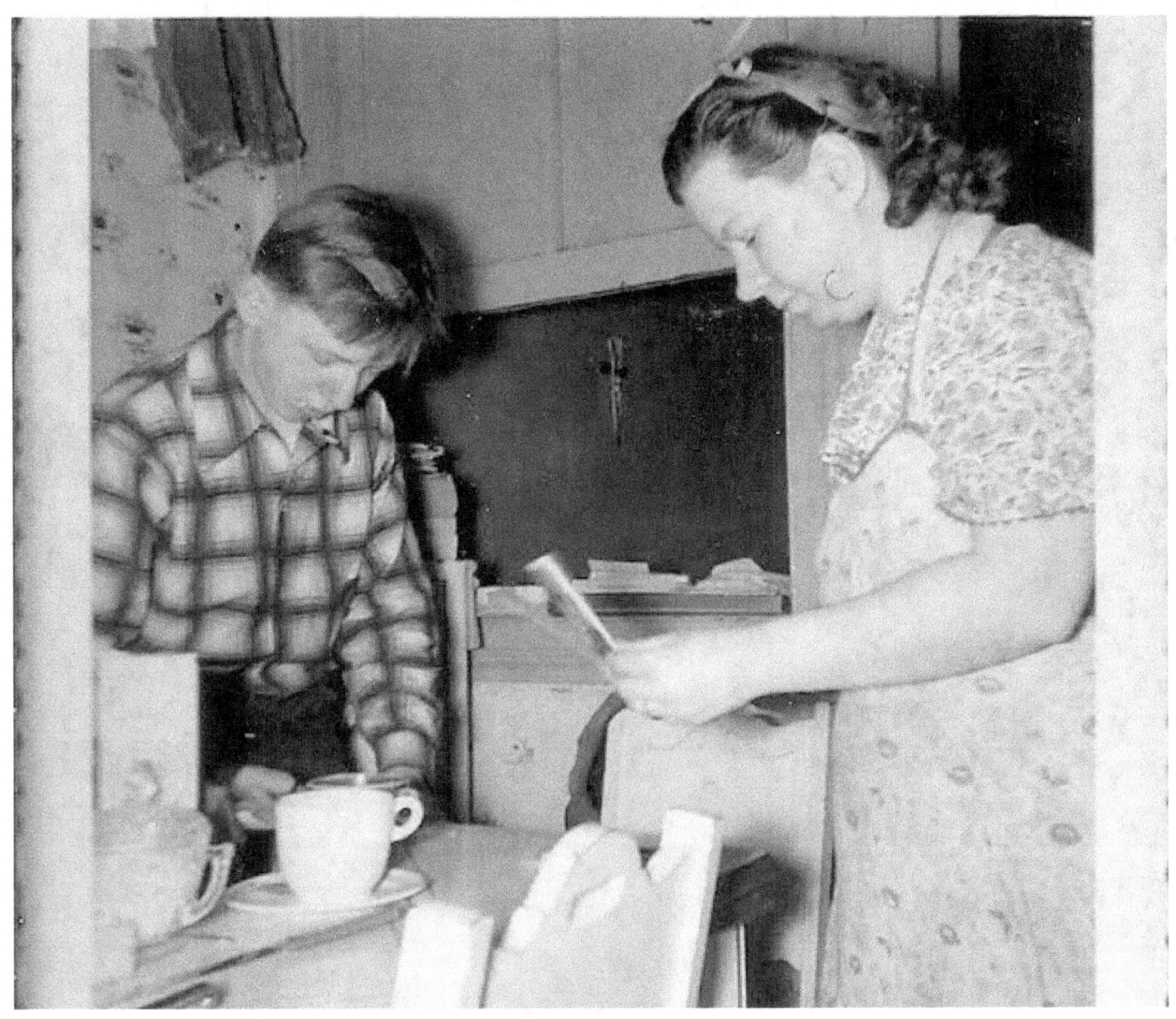

Grandma and Uncle Joe....

Anthony the year I surprised him with a
dell computer...

Dad again

Mom and Dad in N.J.

GRANDPA IN THE ARMY 1944

Sweet picture... 1984

Dad

Grandma and Grandpa....

Uncle Joe...

Christmas 90

Dad age 11

Kassidy and I... Kassidy's 1st birthday

Grandpa's new car.... On Tyram st...

Grandma and Dad in 1986

Dad age 5

Aunt viola...

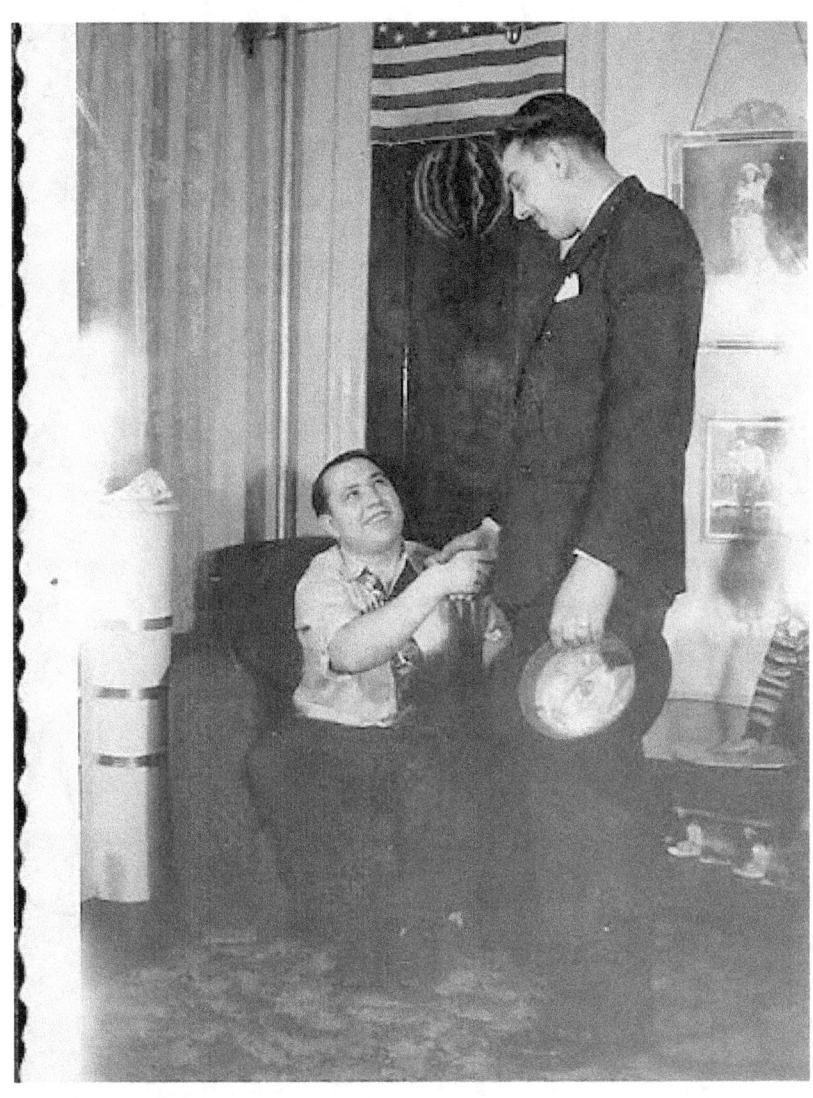

Grandpa and ????????

Again found in grandma's photos don't know who this is....

Another picture found... but don't know
who this is....

I love this one of Grandma and Grandpa...

Anthony, Jocelyn Kassidy and I

Anthony and I when I was carrying second baby☹

Anthony in Fla

Great Grandpa....

Dad and Aunt Maryann...

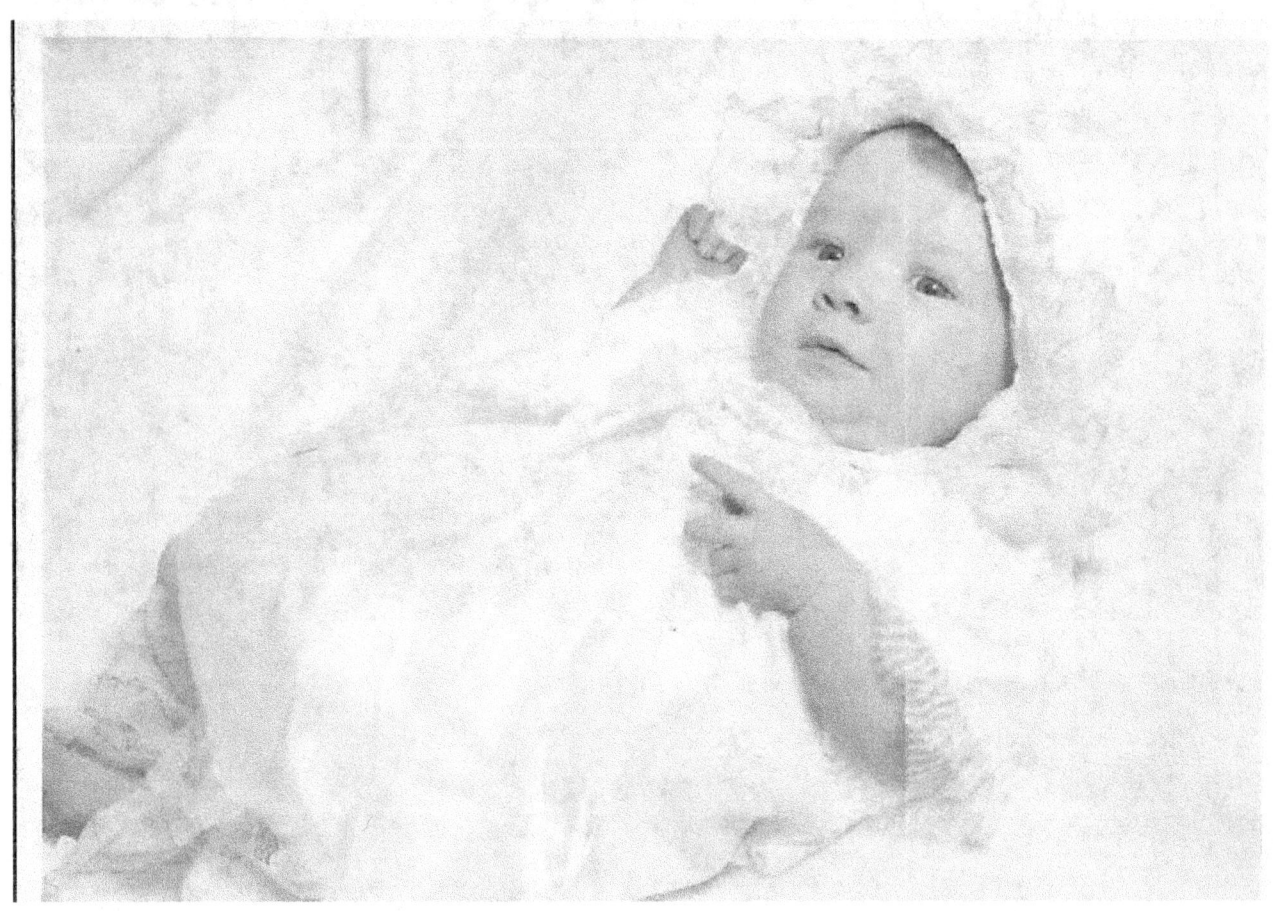

Aunt Maryann....

Dad and I in Atlantic City...

Again dad and Great Grandma in Fl... I
am so amazed by this because Mom never
even know dad went to fl as a little
kid....

Great Grandpa....

Grandpa... I mean um... Santa....

Grandpa at the campsite...

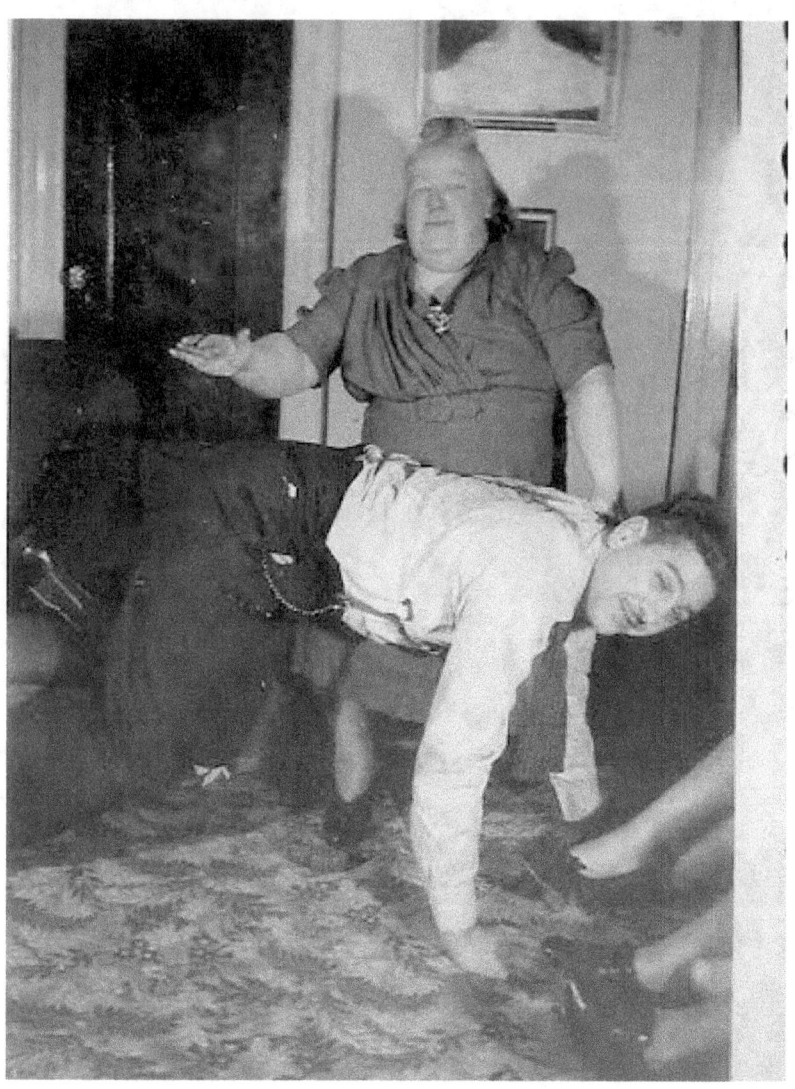

Funny one of Grandpa and Great Grandma

My little angels and I

Wedding

Grandma and Aunt Helen...

Great Grandma

Grandpa and ??????????????

Dad and Aunt Maryann at Lady of the Island....

Brian and Santa

Dad's 1ˢᵗ car....

Grandpa and Dad

DAD

Grandma and Uncle Willie

Grandma and Dad.. the day grandpa came home from war....

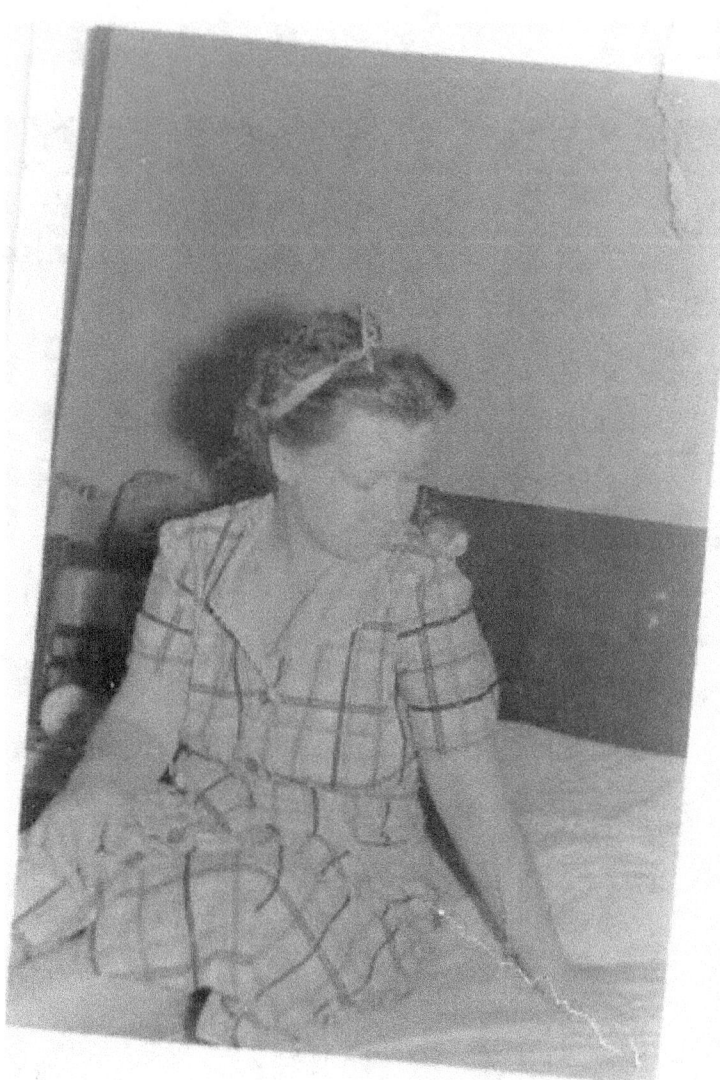

Grandma

The day grandpa came home safely to us..
God bless his service... This picture makes
me cry....

Aunt Mary

DAD

Dad...

Christmas tree 84

Papa got some new shoes....

Dad and Grandpa...

Grandma Christmas 89

Grandma in 47

Grandma and Dad 1942

DAD

Anthony and I

Great Grandpa and Grandma.....

ANTHONY DRESSED AS Santa – Jocelyn is so scared poor baby....

DAD

Dad

Mom and Anthony

Grandpa as a little boy....

A toast to all of YOU!

New Orleans....

Christmas 2013

Grandma and Dad

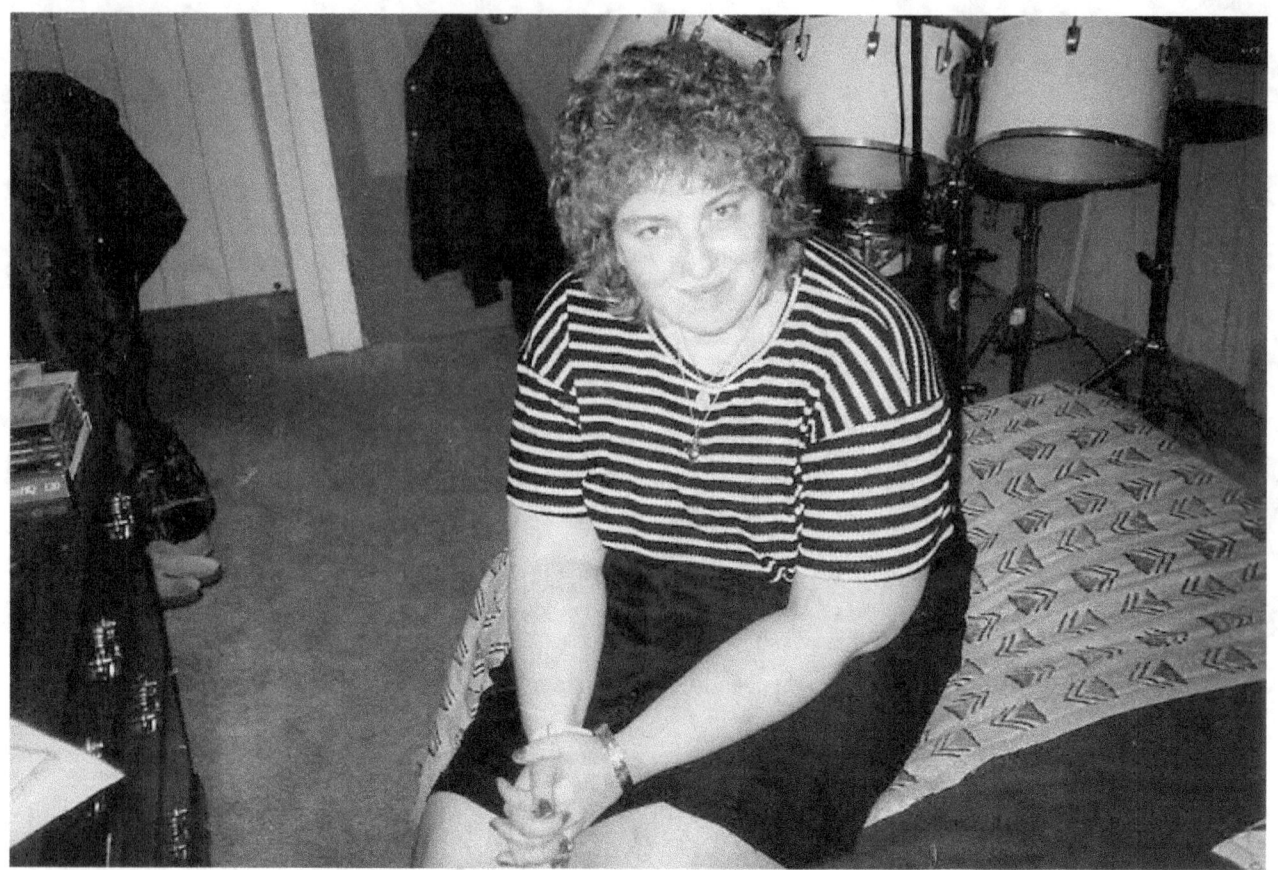

Me

Anthony in 2010

Grandpa

Grandpa....

Dad

Aunt Viola, Aunt Maryann, Dad and Grandpa at dad's grade school

Grandma Aunt Mary and Uncle Charlie?

Dad, Grandma Aunt Viola...

ANTHONY AND i

Love this one....

Mom Anthony and I at Adventureland....

Family bonding time

Grandma dad, Great Grandma and Aunt Viola....

My love and I the day after we got married...

Honeymoon...

Dad and Uncle Joe...

Grandma

DAD

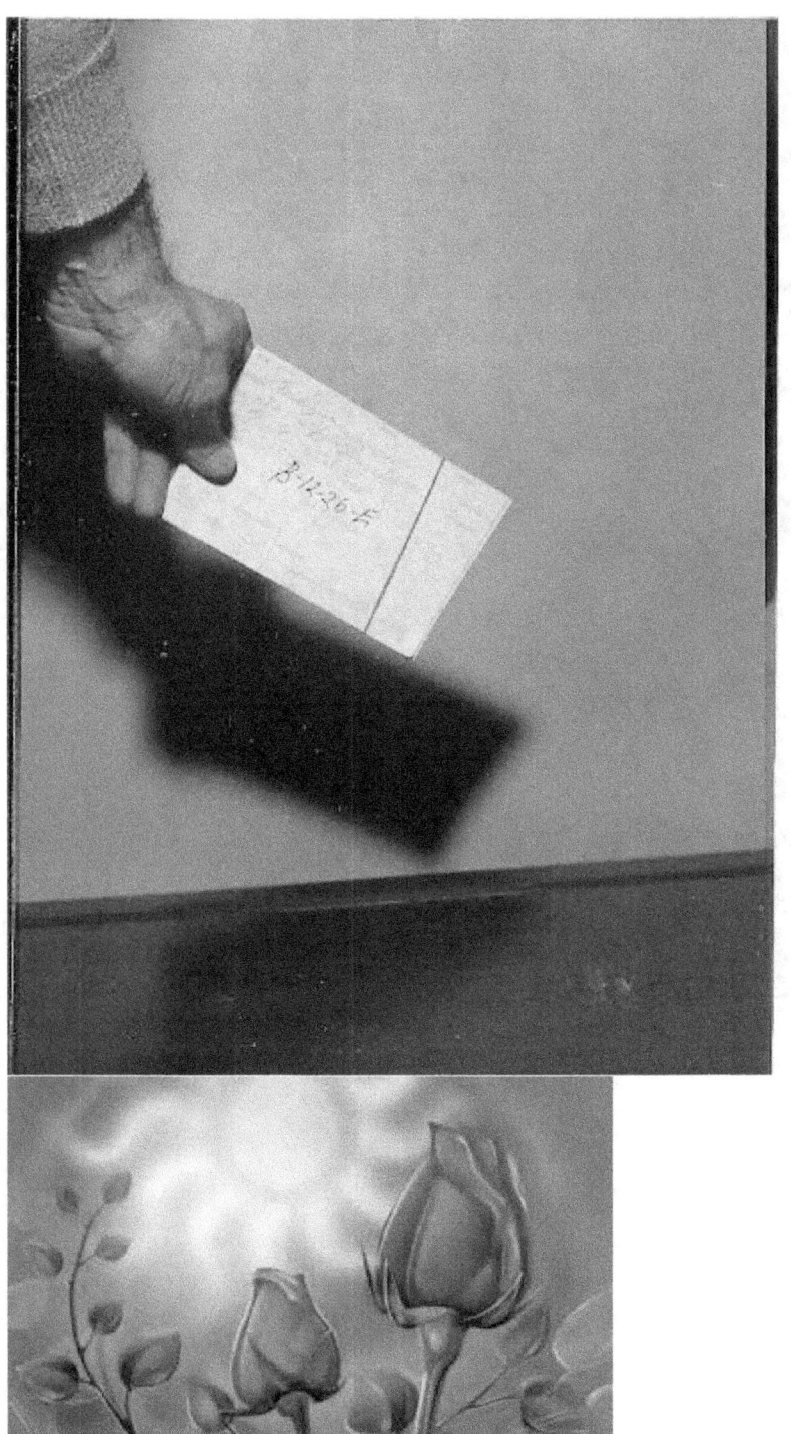

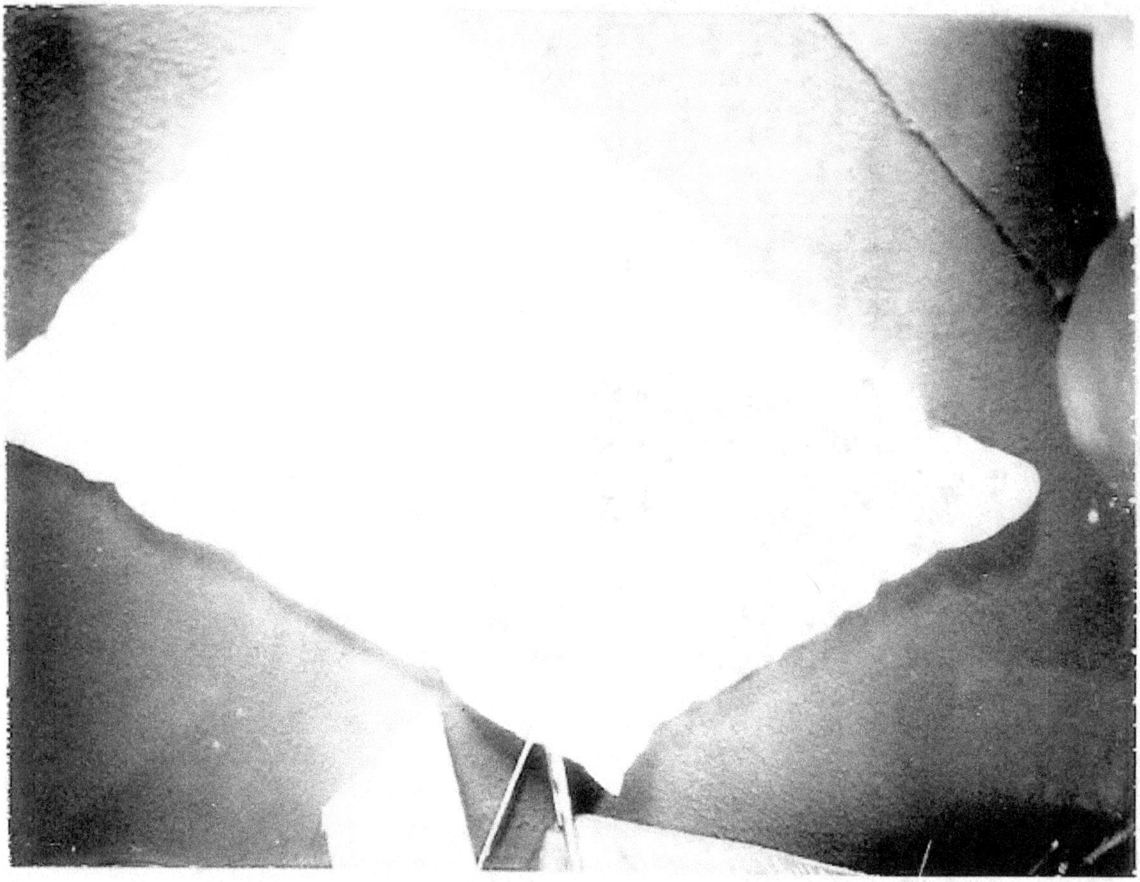

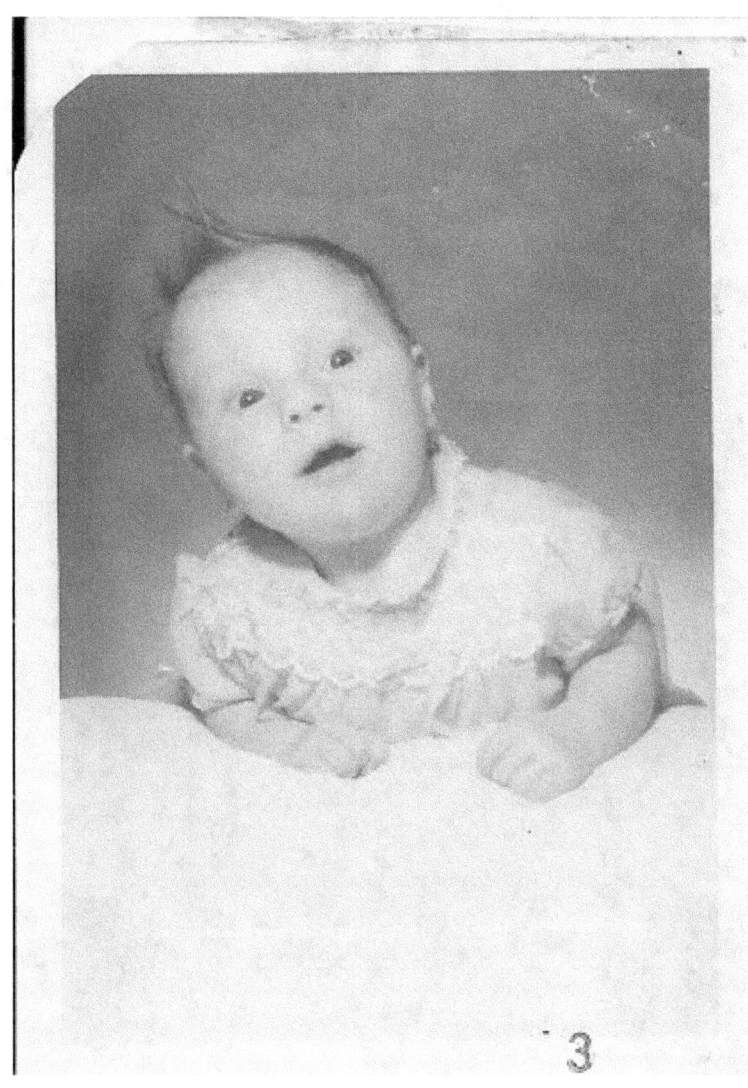

3

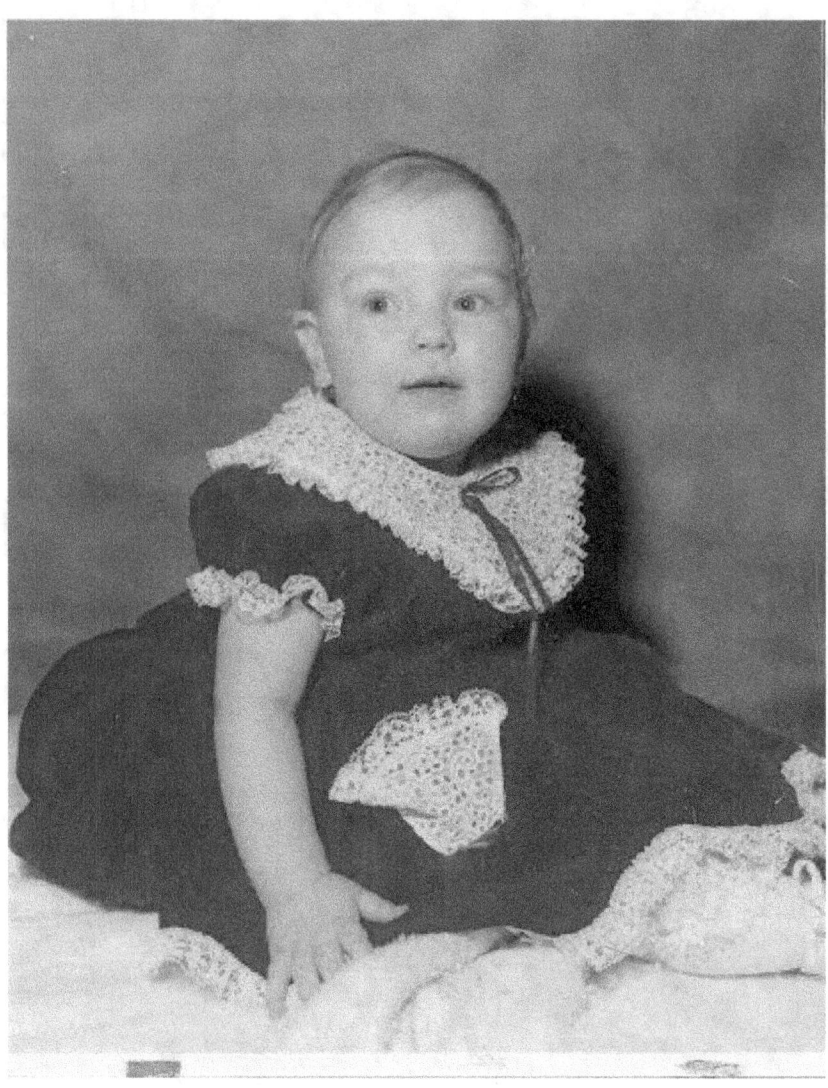

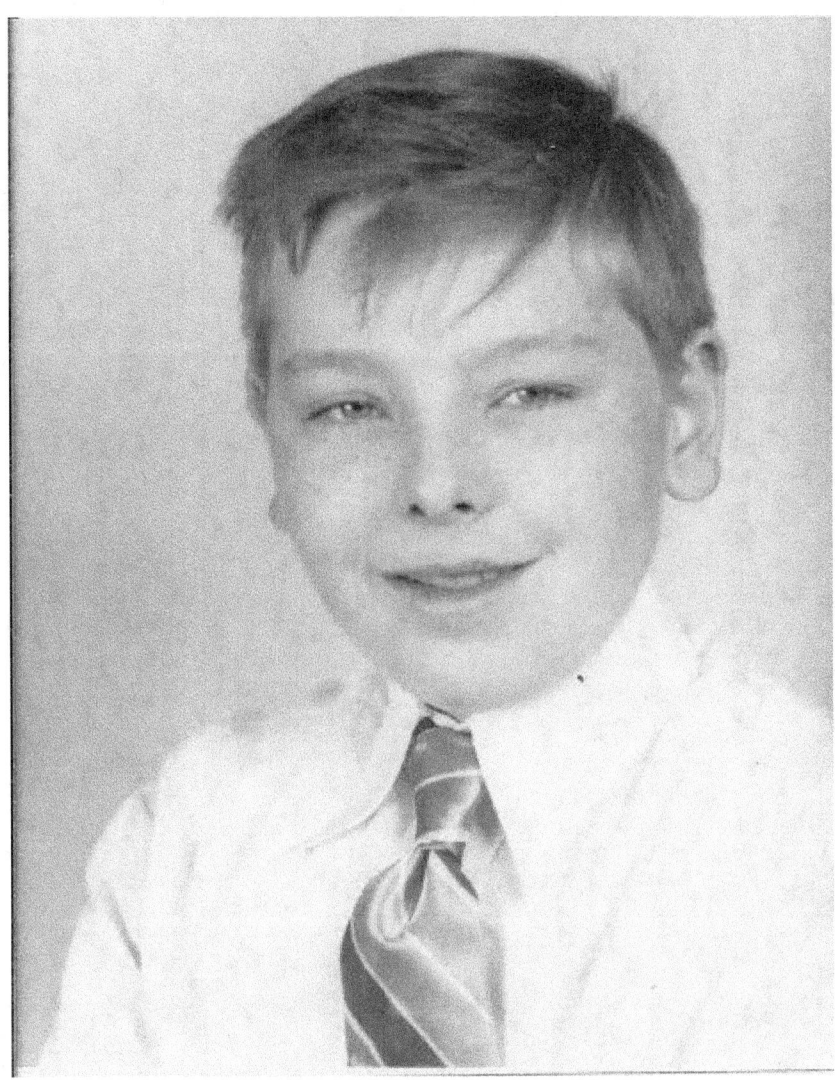

ALWAYS
Thinking Of You

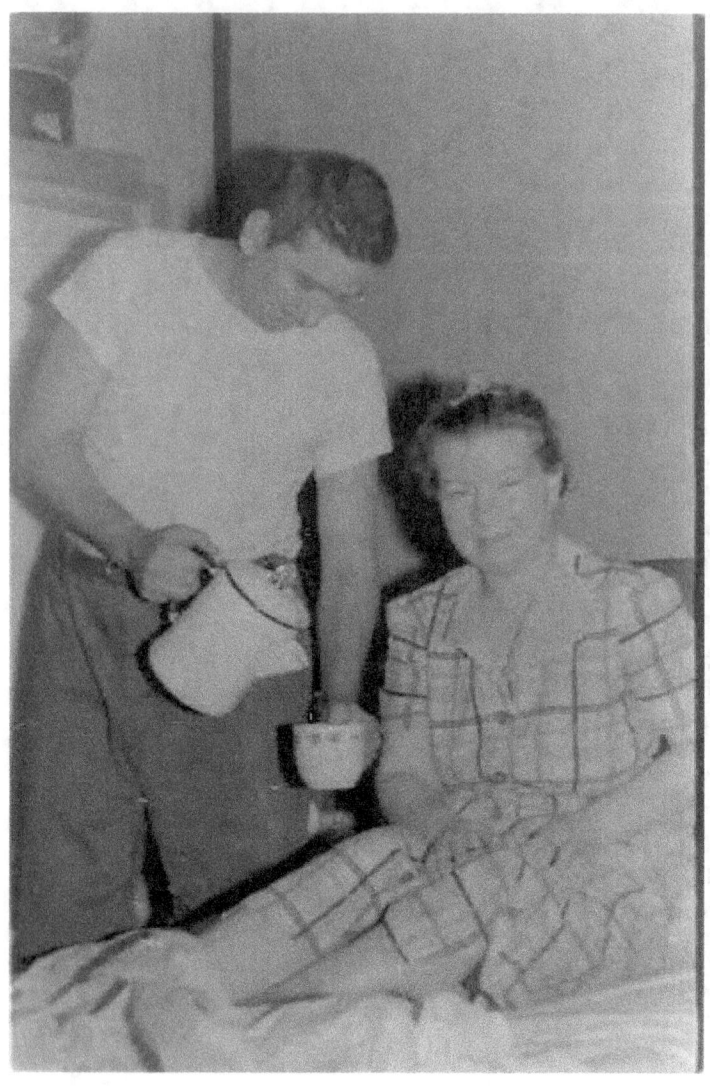

Honestly, I believe in you
Do you trust in me
Patiently, I will stand by you
I will stand beside you faithfully

And through the years
I will be a friend
For always and forever

Call on me and I'll be there for you
I'm a friend who always will be true
And I love you can't you see
That I can say I love you honestly

Call on me and I'll be there for you

I'm a friend who always will be true

And I love you can't you see

That I love you honestly

I will never betray your trust in me

And I love you can't you see

That I can say I love you honestly